The Silk Road

Don Wells

WEIGL PUBLISHERS INC.

Published by Weigl Publishers Inc.
350 5th Avenue, Suite 3304, PMB 6G
New York, NY 10118-0069

Web site: www.weigl.com

All of the Internet URLs given in the book were valid at the time of publication. However, due to
the dynamic nature of the Internet, some addresses may have changed, or sites may have ceased to
exist since publication. While the author and publisher regret any inconvenience this may cause
readers, no responsibility for any such changes can be accepted by either the author or the publisher.

Library of Congress Cataloging-in-Publication Data
Wells, Donald.
 The Silk Road / Donald Wells.
     p. cm. -- (Great journeys)
 Includes index.
 ISBN 1-59036-207-1 (alk. paper) — ISBN 1-59036-260-8 (pbk.)
 1. Silk road--History. 2. Asia--Commerce--History. 3. Asia--Commerce--Europe--History. 4.
Europe--Commerce--Asia--History. I. Title. II. Great journeys (Weigl Publishers)
 DS33.1.W43 2004
 950--dc22

                                             2004002877
                        Printed in the United States of America
                        1 2 3 4 5 6 7 8 9 0   09 08 07 06 05 04

Project Coordinator
Donald Wells
Substantive Editor
Tina Schwartzenberger
Copy Editor
Janice L. Redlin
Photo Researcher
Andrea Harvey
Design & Layout
Bryan Pezzi

Credits
Every reasonable effort has been made to trace ownership and
to obtain permission to reprint copyright material. The publishers
would be pleased to have any errors or omissions brought to their
attention so that they may be corrected in subsequent printings.

Cover: camel and handler on the Silk Road **(Photos.com);**
Corel Corporation: pages 5T, 7, 9, 20; **Bryan Pezzi:** pages 12,
13; **Photos.com:** 1, 4, 5B, 6, 10, 11, 14, 15, 16, 17, 18, 19, 21, 23,
24, 25, 26, 27R; **PhotoSpin Inc.:** page 8; **Jim Steinhart:** page 3;
Ron Watts/CORBIS/MAGMA: page 27L; **Janet Wishnetsky/
CORBIS/MAGMA:** page 22.

**On the Cover:Travelers on the Silk Road crossed the desolate
deserts and mountains of Central Asia to reach China.**

Contents

Bridging East and West

The Silk Road was one of the most important trade routes in the world. For almost 2,000 years (200 BC–AD 1700), traders transported goods along the route from China to countries and empires around the Mediterranean Sea. The Silk Road developed during the **Han Dynasty** (202 BC–AD 220) in China. The route was named in the mid-nineteenth century by German explorer Baron Ferdinand von Richthofen. He named it after the silk cloth that was transported from China to the West.

The Silk Road was not really a road. It was a series of **caravan** tracks that stretched 4,000 miles (6,437 kilometers) across China, Central Asia, Northern India, and the area around the Mediterranean Sea. The Silk Road was made up of three major routes and hundreds of smaller side roads. All of the routes at the eastern end of the road began in Xian, the capital of ancient China. The northern route led from China to the Black Sea. The central route led to Persia—now known as Iran—and the Mediterranean Sea. The southern route took traders through Afghanistan and Persia to India.

Although important for transporting goods between the East and the West, the route's most lasting impact was in the exchange of ideas. Religions such as **Buddhism** traveled along the Silk Road from India through China to Japan. Military leaders, such as Genghis Khan, conquered large parts of the Silk Road and created vast empires.

Silk is the strongest natural fabric in the world. It is used for clothing and to cover furniture and household items, such as pillows and rugs.

Fascinating Fac
The Chinese invented the art of grafting around 2000 BC. Grafting involves uniting parts from two plants so they grow as one.

The Himalayan and Karakourum mountain ranges in Nepal and Pakistan include the world's two highest mountains, Mount Everest and K2.

The Hostile Environment

Travelers on the Chinese end of the Silk Road had to skirt the Taklamakan Desert. This desert has little water and hardly any plants or wildlife. Northeast of this desert is the Gobi Desert, located between Mongolia and China. Travelers on the Silk Road had to pass over the towering Himalayan and Karakourum mountain ranges. Travelers from China had to travel through the Gansu Corridor, a 621-mile (1,000-km) passage between the Mongolian Plateau and the Tibetan High Plateau. Coming from the west or south, travelers made their way through icy passes in the Himalayan and Karakourum mountain ranges.

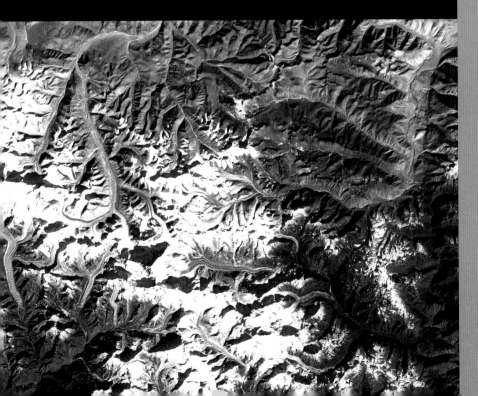

Satellite photos of the Himalayan mountain range show the rough terrain on this part of the Silk Road.

The Desire for Trade

People cannot always produce everything they need or want locally. They often obtain these items through trade. The Silk Road developed from the desire for goods that could not be obtained locally. The western end of the Silk Road developed faster than the eastern end. Empires that could protect travelers and traders from bandits appeared earlier in the West than in the East. Also, the environment was less harsh in the West than in the East. By the time the Greek king Alexander the Great conquered the Middle East early in the third century BC, trade was well established between the Persian Empire in Iran and the kingdoms of India.

China was not part of the Silk Road trade route until the second half of the second century BC. While trying to find allies against their enemy the Xiongnu, a **nomadic** people called Huns, the Han Dynasty in China discovered a group of small kingdoms in Central Asia. These kingdoms had certain trade items the Chinese emperor wanted, such as horses for his cavalry. The Chinese established control of the caravan trails that led to these kingdoms. Once the Chinese had control of the caravan trails, the eastern end of the Silk Road opened for trade with western empires, especially the Roman Empire.

Fascinating Fact
The horses that Zhang Qian brought back from his travels sweated blood. The Chinese believed this was **supernatural**, and they named these horses the "Celestial or Heavenly Horses." This blood was not a supernatural sign. It came from sores caused by parasites under the skin of the horses.

The Father of the Silk Road

In 138 BC, Zhang Qian, a commander of the Chinese imperial guards, left on a dangerous journey. He was sent to form an alliance with the Yueh-chih people who had been forced to move by the Xiongnu. He and his men were captured by the Xiongnu and imprisoned for 10 years. Qian escaped and reached the Yueh-chih people, but they had become settled in a new home and did not want to fight against the Xiongnu. Qian was unable to find any allies. Instead, he returned to China with information about the history, geography, and culture of Central Asia, Persia, Arabia, and the Roman Empire. Han emperor Wu-ti sent trade delegations farther and farther west along the Silk Road as a result of Qian's information.

Islam spread to India along the Silk Road. Jama Masjid is the largest mosque, or Islamic temple, in India.

Boats of the Desert

Caravans on the Silk Road transported silk, tea, and pottery from China to the western regions and pearls, jade, herbal medicines, and perfume from Central and West Asia and Europe to China. The animal most commonly used in caravans was the camel because it did not need to drink water for several days and could carry heavy loads. The camel became known as the "boat of the desert."

The two-humped Bactrian camel was most often used in ancient caravans. The Bactrian camel could carry 400 to 500 pounds (181–227 kilograms) of merchandise 15 to 30 miles (24–48 km) a day. If the weather was hot, caravans would travel at night. Camels do not like hot weather.

In some areas, the camel was harnessed to a cart. Usually, the load was divided into two parts and secured on either side of the camel's back. Passengers were carried in large wicker baskets slung on each side of the camel.

Up to forty camels were fastened together in strings. A rope attached to a camel's nose ring was tied to the saddle of the camel in front. Three or four strings of camels might travel side by side in a caravan. Sometimes, camels would travel in one long line.

Camels also wore bells. If the rope came untied, the camel could be found by listening for the sound of its bell.

Camels are loyal companions and guides to desert travelers. Camels often guide travelers to water.

Fascinating Fact
Camels are very timid. Even a rabbit will frighten a camel. The bell worn by a camel warns animals, such as rabbits, to hide so camels will not be disturbed.

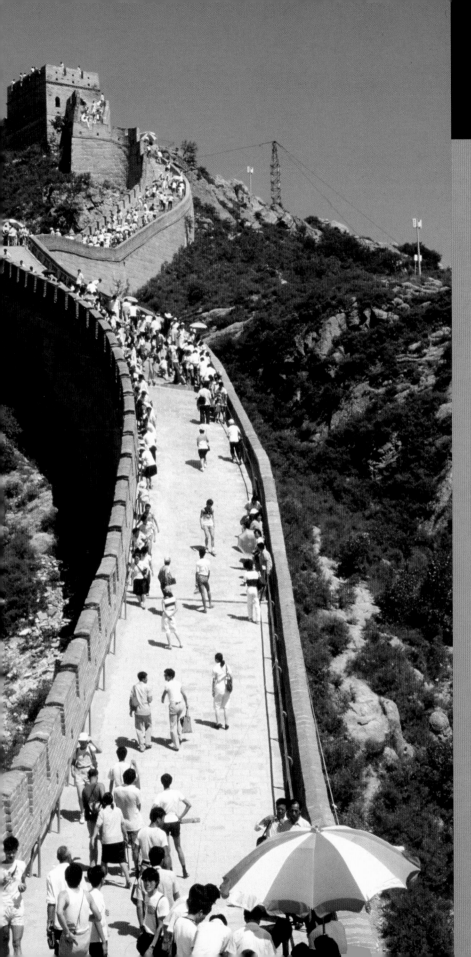

How Willows Protected Silk Road Caravans

Around 200 BC, the Chinese began to trade with the West, particularly Rome. The Chinese and trade caravans were under attack from nomadic tribes. The Chinese repaired and strengthened the Great Wall to protect the caravans. They also added 298 miles (465 km) to the Great Wall in the Gobi Desert.

The Gobi Desert portion of the Wall was built with packed earth. Branches of red willow were laid in the soil, and water was added before the soil was packed. In the dry environment, the willow reinforced the packed soil.

This type of construction was very successful. Sections of this part of the Great Wall still remain in the Gobi Desert.

The Great Wall of China attracts millions of visitors each year.

An Ancient Chain

The Silk Road flourished because silk, which was produced only in China until AD 300, and other luxury goods from the East were very popular with Romans. Along the eastern section of the Silk Road, the Chinese traded silk and other goods with Central Asian traders and merchants. These traders transported silk and luxury goods, such as tea, by caravan through the **oasis** towns of Central Asia. In the oasis town markets, traders exchanged silk for goods, such as glass and wool, brought by traders from western cities such as Rome. Persian, Armenian, and Jewish traders transported the silk and other eastern goods through Persia to Rome. Roman citizens purchased the silk and other eastern goods with gold.

Trade on the Silk Road resembled a chain, with each trader and segment of the trade route representing a crucial link in this chain. The trading that occurred along each trade route segment was known as peddling trade. A trader sold goods and bought other goods while traveling from one market to another. Sometimes, traders exchanged goods without using money. This is called bartering. For example, a Middle-Eastern trader might travel eastward with goods unavailable in Central Asia or China, such as colored glass or white jade. These goods were traded for a profit, and other goods, such as silk, were purchased for resale in the West.

Drinking tea is said to have originated when a leaf fell from a wild tea tree into the Emperor of China's boiling water.

An Information Superhighway

People along the Silk Road also traded culture. They heard different types of music, viewed different styles of art, and learned about different religions. Technologies, such as papermaking and glass making, were exchanged between the Chinese and people in the Mediterranean area. Pilgrims and monks traveled along the trade routes and spread their religious beliefs. By the fourth century AD, Buddhism had spread from India to China. Christian sects reached China by AD 638 and remained until the fourteenth century. **Manichaeism** from Persia, **Judaism** from the Middle East, and **Confucianism** from China also spread along the Silk Road. Eventually, Islam from Arabia became the dominant religion from the Middle East to the northern border of China.

Buddhism spread along the Silk Road and reached Japan in the late sixth century AD.

oday, the Silk Road is a series of paved roads and train tracks that follow the paths of the old routes. These roads and railroads are in poor condition. As a result, an Asian Highway project has been proposed that would recreate the old Silk Road. This project will include an 87,000-mile (140,000-km) web of highways and ferry routes that will connect Asia and Europe.

BLACK SEA

CASPIAN SEA

New Sarai

Antioch

Damascus

Ecbatane

Jerusalem

Bagdad

Babylon

RED SEA

Seleucia

● Medina

● Mecca

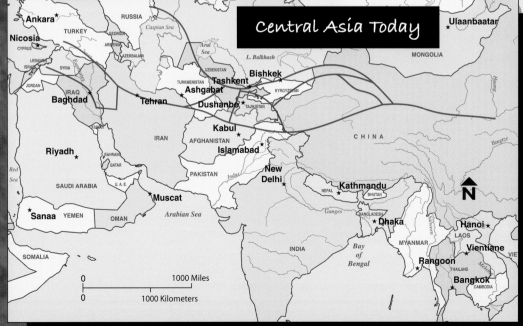

Central Asia Today

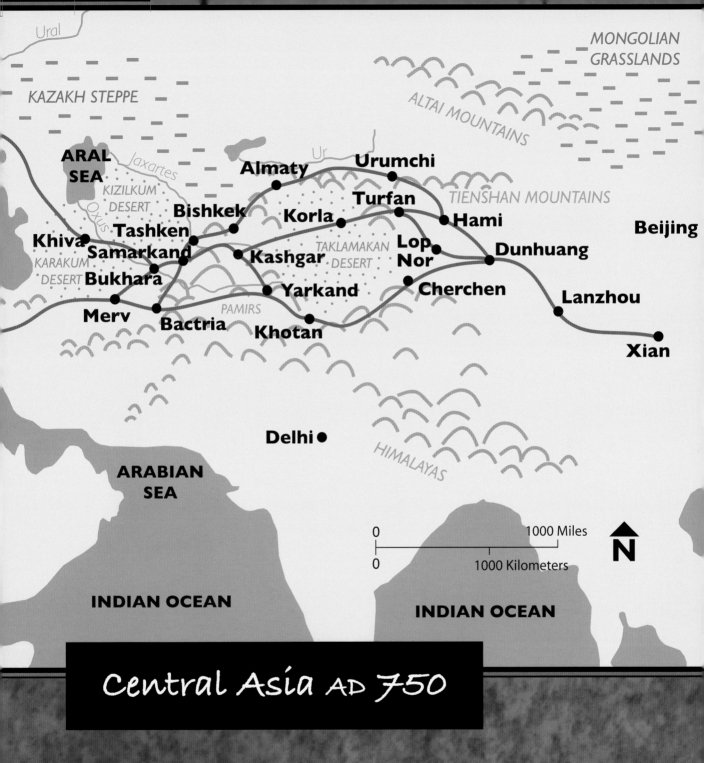

Central Asia AD 750

Conflict and Peace

Successful trade on the Silk Road depended on peace and stability. There were three periods of relative peace on the Silk Road—the Han Dynasty (202 BC–AD 220), the Tang Dynasty (AD 618–907), and the Mongol Empire (AD 1206–1368).

During the Han Dynasty, the Chinese extended the length of the Great Wall to protect caravans on the eastern end of the Silk Road. When the Han Dynasty collapsed, bandits found it easier to attack caravans on the Silk Road. Trade did not stop completely, but it did not flourish again until the Tang Dynasty came to power in China. The Tang Dynasty provided security for caravans on the eastern end of the Silk Road. When the Tang Dynasty fell, trade once again suffered. During the thirteenth century, the Mongols conquered most of the territory covered by the Silk Road. The Mongols created a peaceful environment that allowed people such as Marco Polo to travel safely along the trade route. As the Mongol Empire's power declined, the Silk Road again became a dangerous trade route.

Despite the stability created by the Chinese and Mongol empires, there were occasional battles between local governments trying to keep control of their part of the Silk Road. By the fifteenth century, sea routes from Europe to Asia had become established. These safer, quicker routes reduced the need to transport goods over the long and sometimes dangerous Silk Road.

The first Chinese Emperor Qin Shihuangdi (221–210 BC) was buried with more than 8,000 terra cotta soldiers. Chinese soldiers such as these fought hand-to-hand combat until the invention of gunpowder in the ninth century AD.

Genghis Khan's Mongol warriors wore armor made of boiled leather.

Bandits on the Silk Road

Raiding parties of bandits sometimes attacked caravans on the Silk Road. Han, Tang, and Mongol dynasty armies protected caravans from raiders in northern China. When merchants traveled in areas without strong armies, they often worked together. They formed large caravans to discourage bandits from attacking. Wealthier merchants hired bodyguards to defend their lives and property. Buddhists, Christians, Muslims, Jews, and others prayed for protection from brutal attacks by bandits. Some people even believed evil spirits would attack them on the Silk Road. Many traders refused to leave the bazaars, or markets, in oasis towns because of the great risks involved in traveling on the Silk Road.

Fascinating Fact
The Mongol rulers developed a postal relay system that operated on the Silk Road. The system was similar to the pony express in the American West. Couriers carrying messages for the Khan, or ruler, could show their badge of authority and receive fresh horses at regularly placed relay stations.

New Inventions

The Silk Road affected people's lives. It affected those who lived along the route. It affected those who eventually received the goods traded on it. Local people profited from trade by catering to the needs of passing traders. Local governments charged foreign traders taxes when they passed through their regions. These taxes raised so much money that wars were fought to control trade along different sections of the Silk Road.

New ideas and inventions were transported along the Silk Road and affected life in the East and West. For example, the Chinese invented the moveable printing press in 1045. Johannes Gutenberg, a German printer, built an improved printing press in 1436. Gutenberg's printing press helped spread knowledge. Printing made it easier to produce more copies of old books and an increasing number of new books. Cheaper, more available written material helped Europeans enter the **Renaissance** (1450–1600). During this period, European art, politics, science, and society turned in new directions that led to modern ideas such as democracy.

The development of cannons in the West is linked to the Chinese invention of gunpowder. Cannons made castles obsolete because cannonballs could blast holes through castle walls. Armor could not protect knights against men who carried guns. This changed the nature of warfare and forced armies to devise new ways to wage war.

Fascinating Fact
Paper money was first used in China in the ninth century AD. Its original name was "flying money." It was so light it could blow out of a person's hand.

The compass guided fifteenth-century Portuguese explorers around the tip of Africa. It helped them open up the first all-sea route from Western Europe to the ports of East Africa and Asia.

The Black Death on the Silk Road

Traveling by ships saved time and was much safer than traveling along the Silk Road.

The Black Death plague that devastated Europe in the fourteenth century is believed to have traveled along the Silk Road from Central Asia. The Black Death changed European society. The **feudal system** in Europe began to collapse because of a worker shortage caused by people dying from the plague. The common people, called serfs, began working for those who offered the highest wages. Kings and nobles had to pay professional soldiers to fight in their armies. These paid soldiers replaced serfs who had to serve in their lord's army for no pay. Landowners and nobles lost power as they lost their wealth. The combination of the nobles' loss of power, the demands for money to pay soldiers and peasants, and the destruction of the peasant labor force destroyed the feudal system. All this created the foundation for modern society.

Marco Polo

Marco Polo (AD 1254–1324) is the best-known traveler on the Silk Road. Marco Polo was born in 1254 in Venice, Italy, a trade city. In 1262, his father and uncle traveled to the court of Kublai Khan in China. Kublai Khan was a powerful ruler who controlled most of the land on the eastern end of the Silk Road. Kublai Khan's rule over China and a large portion of Central Asia made it safe for people to travel the entire Silk Road.

Marco Polo was 17 years old when his father and uncle returned to Italy. In 1271, Marco Polo's father and uncle took Marco with them on a trip to China. After more than 3 years traveling the Silk Road, the Polos reached China.

Kublai Khan was particularly interested in meeting Marco. He enjoyed listening to Marco's stories, and Marco quickly gained the ruler's favor. Kublai Khan sent Marco on government trips all over China. On his travels, Marco was fascinated by many Chinese inventions, such as paper money, printing machines, and coal fuel, which did not exist in Europe. Marco stayed in China for 17 years before he returned to Venice.

Marco Polo described his adventures in his book *The Travels of Marco Polo or A Description of the World.*

Three years after returning to Venice, Marco Polo fought in a war against the rival city of Genoa.

Genghis Khan

Genghis Khan was born in the 1160s. His father, Yesugi, was the leader of a small **clan** in northeastern Mongolia. When Genghis Khan was 9 years old, his father died. After his father's death, Genghis Khan worked for his father's brother, Toghril Khan. Toghril was Mongolia's most powerful leader at the time.

The Mongols believed that one day Genghis Khan would rise again and lead his people to new victories.

Genghis Khan became a skilled military leader. He developed a new military system. His armies were split into groups of 10, 100, 1,000, and 10,000. Soldiers had three or four horses, so they always had fresh transportation. Genghis Khan attacked without mercy. His only goal was to conquer anyone who opposed him. Genghis Khan's opponents had to choose between becoming slaves or dying.

Genghis Khan united the different Mongol clans. He convinced Mongolian leaders to serve Mongolia instead of their own clans. Genghis Khan ruled his empire from 1206 to 1227. His empire stretched from Hungary across Asia to Korea and from Siberia to Tibet. At the time of his death in 1227, Genghis Khan ruled over one of the largest empires in history.

Life on the Silk Road

Traders or merchants who wished to make a profit from trading at the different centers along the Silk Road would organize a trade expedition. The trader saved or borrowed money to make the trip. Once the money had been obtained, the route had to be selected. Each route had advantages and disadvantages. Some routes were dangerous. Other routes took longer to travel. Choosing the correct route was very important to the success of the trade expedition. If one section of the route was plagued by bandits or was impassable because of the weather, the trader would have to change routes. This could delay the trip. If the trip was delayed, the trader might make less profit.

Fascinating Fact
Experienced traders on the Silk Road were known by the Persian word *rahdanan*, which means "people who know the roads," or "roadies."

Traders often traveled in a caravan. When the caravan reached a town, it would go to a *caravanserai*, a special place for traders to stay and leave their animals. The traders ate, drank, and socialized together. They exchanged stories about different regions and travel conditions along the Silk Road.

Two popular destinations were Bactria—located in what is now known as Afghanistan—and Samarkand—a city in what is now known as Uzbekistan. These areas were filled with many marketplaces. Traders from different regions bartered with and sold their goods to local merchants in these marketplaces.

There were between 200 and 300 camels in the average caravan traveling on the Silk Road.

The Caravanserai

Caravanserais were places where caravans stopped to rest. In some cases, the caravanserais were oasis cities. They also were fortified inns located along trade routes. In the eleventh century AD, the rulers of Iran established caravanserais every 19 to 25 miles (30–40 km), a distance that could be traveled on foot in 8 to 10 hours. The caravanserai offered traders a safe place to spend the night on remote roads. Iranian caravanserais were operated by wealthy people or charitable foundations. These caravanserais did not charge travelers a fee. Regardless of their religion, language, or race, travelers were given a room for 3 days, their animals were taken care of and fed, and the sick were cared for free of charge.

Silk Road travelers had to cross a range of sand dunes in the Taklamakan Desert that is 25 miles (40 km) long and 5,627 feet (1,715 meters) high.

The following is an excerpt from a merchant's handbook called *Pratica della Mercatura*. This merchant's handbook was written by Francesco Balducci Pegolotti, an Italian merchant, around AD 1340. At this time, the Mongol Empire was still providing protection to travelers and traders on the Silk Road. Pegolotti describes the relative security of trade routes through the territories of the Mongol Empire and the variety of products available in commercial centers along the Silk Road.

The ruins of ancient caravanserais can be seen along the Silk Road today.

In the first place, you must let your beard grow long and not shave. And at Tana (in what is now known as the Ukraine) you should furnish yourself with a **dragoman**. And you must not try to save money in the matter of dragomen by taking a bad one instead of a good one. For the additional wages of the good one will not cost you so much as you will save by having him. And besides the dragoman it will be well to take at least two good men servants, who are acquainted with the Cumanian, or Tartar, tongue.

And from Tana traveling to Gittarchan (in what is now known as Russia on the Volga River) you should take with you twenty-five days' provisions, that is to say, flour and salt fish, for as to meat you will find enough of it at all the places along the road.

The road you travel from Tana to Cathay (China) is perfectly safe, whether by day or by night, according to what the merchants say who have used it. Only if the merchant, in going or coming, should die upon the road, everything belonging to him will become the perquisite of the lord of the country in which he dies, and the officers of the lord will take possession of all. And in like manner if he die in Cathay. But if his brother be with him, or an intimate friend and comrade calling himself his brother, then to such an one they will surrender the property of the deceased, and so it will be rescued.

And there is another danger: this is when the lord of the country dies, and before the new lord who is to have the lordship is proclaimed; there have sometimes been irregularities practiced on the Franks (Christians), and other foreigners. And neither will the roads be safe to travel until the other lord be proclaimed who is to reign in room of him who is deceased.

The Silk Road Today

Today, the Silk Road is regaining importance. Road construction and the discovery of large oil and gas reserves under the desert are encouraging development in Central Asia. Tourism is a growing industry in the Central Asian countries of Kazakhstan, Kyrgyzstan, Turkmenistan, and Uzbekistan. The trade route is also being reopened. The recent trend toward a **market economy** in China is encouraging trade. Since China allowed foreign tourists to visit at the end of the 1970s, tourism has become a profitable industry for the Chinese. This has encouraged Chinese authorities to protect and restore the remaining historical sites along its section of the Silk Road.

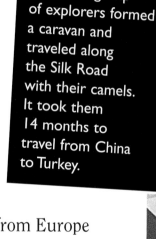

Fascinating Fact
In 1997, a group of explorers formed a caravan and traveled along the Silk Road with their camels. It took them 14 months to travel from China to Turkey.

This ancient trade route has seen many changes over the past 2,000 years. Trade on the Silk Road has always depended on the political stability of Central Asia. Strong empires, such as the Mongol Empire, provided traders with safe routes from China to the

West. As these empires fell and safer, quicker sea routes from Europe to Asia opened in the fifteenth century, trade on the Silk Road slowly declined. Today, the political climate in Central Asia is once again becoming stable. As a result of this stability, the Silk Road may see international trade once again. This time, however, trade may take place on a scale never thought possible in the days of traveling by camels and horses.

Today, China has a population of approximately 1.2 billion people.

Space-age Technology and the Silk Road

Many cities along the Silk Road have disappeared under desert sands. The climate in Central Asia has become drier over the past 2,000 years. These drier conditions forced people to abandon their cities and move closer to water supplies. Space-age **technology** is helping archeologists search for the lost cities on China's ancient Silk Road. Data from NASA's *Spaceborne Imaging Radar*, or *SIR-C*, which flew on the space shuttle twice in 1994, is being used to study the Taklamakan Desert in China's dry northwest. Radar imagery can see through fine, dry sand. The technology promises to help explorers find lost cities among the Taklamakan's shifting sand dunes.

Images taken from space help scientists learn more about life on the Silk Road.

Goods were transported along the Silk Road between China and civilizations in the west. People from different cultures traveled with these goods, bringing with them new ideas and inventions. The West received technology that helped create modern society, such gunpowder. Buddhism and new ideas about art were the most important innovations the Chinese received from the West.

One famous example of a Chinese invention that helped transform the world is paper. Paper was invented during the Han Dynasty, around the time the Silk Road trade began to flourish. Far superior to the narrow wooden strips or hard-to-handle rolls of silk that the Chinese had used for writing, paper soon became the writing material of choice throughout China and East Asia. Paper was also found in northwestern China's Buddhist temples. Paper became important in the West after AD 1453, when Johannes Gutenberg invented the moveable printing press. Within 50 years of the invention of Gutenberg's printing press, 500,000 religious texts were printed. Within 100 years, academic works and works of fiction were being printed. Gutenberg's printing press and paper from China helped spread knowledge throughout Europe.

Fascinating Fact
The Chinese developed the process to refine iron into steel in the second century BC.

The earliest known printed book is the *Diamond Sutra*, a Buddhist holy text. It was printed in AD 868.

Matches

The Chinese were very successful inventors in ancient times. They invented the wheelbarrow, irrigation systems, and the umbrella. In AD 577, they invented matches. Early Chinese matches were little sticks of pinewood soaked with **sulfur**. At the slightest touch, they burst into flame. At first, matches were called "light-bringing slaves." When matches became a trade item, they were called "fire inch-sticks." Matches were not used in Europe until 1530, almost 1,000 years after the Chinese invented them. However, a few matches may have reached parts of Europe during the time of Marco Polo. Matches were being sold in some Chinese cities when Polo visited China.

A modern-day printing press can print millions of copies of one page in a single day.

Time Line

3000 BC
China breeds silkworms and produces silk.

300 BC
Bactrian camels are used to transport goods and people in the desert.

200 BC
The Silk Road opens for the trade of silk and other goods.

AD 1
Silk is first seen in Rome. Silk garments quickly become fashionable.

100
Buddhism reaches China.

300s
Silk cloth is woven throughout Asia using silk thread purchased from China.

400s
The secret of silk making leaks out along the Silk Road's westward route.

600s
Silkworm farms are built in Europe.

638
Christianity reaches China.

800s
Islam begins to spread in Central Asia. After capturing papermaking craftsmen in China, the Arabs introduce papermaking skills into Central Asia and Europe.

1200s (early)
Seagoing trade begins to replace overland commerce on the Silk Road. Italy establishes its own silk production and weaving.

1200s
Islam swiftly envelopes much of Central Asia.

1206
The Mongols conquer China. Products and ideas flow more freely along the Silk Road.

1400s
Better ships and new sea routes offer more efficient and safer trade by sea than by land. Europeans learn the art of producing silk.

1870s
The term *Silk Road* is coined by German explorer Baron Ferdinand von Richthofen.

Activity: Making a Simple Compass

The Chinese invented a simple compass in the third century BC. Chinese sailors first used the compass to navigate by sea in the ninth century AD. It did not appear in Europe until 1190. The compass enabled sailors to explore distant lands and find their way back home.

What you need:

- sewing needle or straight pin 1 inch (2.5 centimeters) long
- small magnet
- small cork used for fishing (or a piece of a larger one)
- small cup or saucer of water

How to make the compass:

1. First, magnetize the needle or pin by "stroking" the needle or pin with the magnet. Holding the magnet the same way each time, place it in contact with the pin, and run it down the length of the pin. Lift the magnet up, return to the starting point, and stroke it again. Always stroke the pin or needle in the same direction with the same part of the magnet.

2. Place the cork in the cup of water to see how it sits in the water. The magnet you used was probably not very strong, so a smaller piece of cork works best. A small circular piece of cork cut off a fishing cork will work well. Ask an adult to help you cut the cork. Force the needle all the way through the cork so that it sticks out above the water on both sides.

3. Float the cork and pin in the water. The needle should stick out of the water parallel to the surface. Watch what happens as the ripples in the water stop. The pin will slowly begin to turn until it is pointing along the north/south axis of Earth. The manner in which you held the magnet will determine whether the pin's head or tip points to the North Pole. You now have a compass that can be used anywhere you can find a puddle of water deep enough to float the cork.

4. Earth's magnetic field is not very strong. As long as you keep the weight of the pin/cork combination low and let it move freely on the surface of the water, it will align itself with Earth's magnetic field.

1. Who is considered to be the father of the Silk Road?

2. Name two deserts on the Silk Road.

3. What type of camel was most often used to transport goods on the Silk Road?

4. Why was the Great Wall of China built?

5. What is bartering?

6. Who controlled most of the Silk Road when Marco Polo traveled to China in the 1300s?

7. The Black Death traveled to Europe from which part of the world?

8. What was a caravanserai?

9. Name one reason the Silk Road is once again becoming important?

10. Who invented matches, and when were they invented?

Answers on page 32.

Answers on page 32.

Web sites
www.asiasociety.org/arts/ monksandmerchants
This Web site contains interesting information about different aspects of the Silk Road.

www.cps.ci.cambridge.ma.us/ element/Tobin/directory/ Grade6/silkroad/silkroad.html
This Web site is a great source of links to other Web sites about the history of the Silk Road, Chinese inventions, the history of silk, and other subjects related to the Silk Road.

www.silk-road.com/artl/ marcopolo.shtml
This Web site contains a detailed description of Marco Polo's life.

Books
Bailey, L. and B. Slavin. *Adventures in Ancient China*. Toronto: Kids Can Press, 2003.

Herbert, J. *Marco Polo for Kids*. Chicago: Chicago Review Press, 2001.

Glossary

Buddhism: a religion of Eastern and Central Asia growing out of the teaching of Gautama Buddha

caravan: a group of traders crossing the desert together for safety, usually with a train of camels

clan: a group of people related by blood or marriage

Confucianism: the ethical teachings of the Chinese philosopher Confucius

dragoman: a translator or guide

feudal system: the European social system in which commoners called serfs were protected by lords they had to serve in war

Han Dynasty: a series of powerful leaders in the same family that ruled China from 202 BC to AD 220

Islam: religion founded in Arabia in the seventh century and based on the teachings of Muhammad as laid down in the *Koran*, Islam's sacred book

Judaism: a religion developed among the ancient Hebrews and characterized by belief in one God

Manichaeism: a religion based on the idea that the body is evil and the mind is good; originated in third-century Persia

market economy: economy based on the production of goods and services for sale

nomadic: having no fixed home and moving according to the seasons from place to place in search of food, water, and grazing land

oasis: a place in the desert where there is water

Renaissance: the period from the fourteenth to sixteenth centuries that marks the transition from medieval to modern times

sulfur: a pale yellow element that exists in various physical forms; burns with a blue flame and has a strong smell; is used in medicine and industry

supernatural: cannot be explained by the laws of nature

technology: the practical application of knowledge

Index

Answers to Quiz on Page 30
1. Zhang Qian 2. the Gobi Desert and the Taklamakan Desert. 3. the two-humped Bactrian camel 4. to defend against attacks from nomadic tribes 5. Traders exchange goods for other goods without the use of money. 6. the Mongols 7. Central Asia 8. a special place where traders could rest and leave their animals 9. the discovery of oil and gas in Central Asia, road construction, or tourism 10. The Chinese invented matches in AD 577.